AF512294

The Global Foodie

Aalok Wadhwa

Popular Prakashan
www.popularprakashan.com

Published by
POPULAR PRAKASHAN PVT. LTD.
301, Mahalaxmi Chambers
22, Bhulabhai Desai Road
Mumbai – 400 026

First Published 2009

(4307)
ISBN – 978-81-7991-559-2

Design: Quadrant Infotech (India) Pvt. Ltd

Printed in India
by New Model Impex Pvt. Ltd.
New Delhi - 110055

Contents

Salads 25–36

Vegetables 37–58

Meat, Chicken and Seafood 59–82

Appetizers

Guacamole Dip

Method

1. Mix all the ingredients together and mash with a fork until the avocado is almost dissolved.
2. Serve with corn chips.

Ingredients

- 2 avocados, peeled and sliced
- 1 tomato, diced
- ½ onion, diced
- 1 jalapeno pepper, diced
- ¼ tsp salt
- 1 tbsp chopped fresh coriander leaves
- Corn chips, to serve

Chicken Satay

Ingredients

- 550 gms boneless chicken breast, cut into ½" wide strips
- 1 tbsp curry powder*
- ½ tsp coriander powder
- ¼ tsp turmeric powder
- A pinch of red chilli powder
- Salt to taste
- 1 tsp peanut oil
- 1 tsp water
- 8 thin metal or bamboo skewers

**Garam Masala*

Method

1. Place the chicken strips in a bowl and add the curry, coriander, turmeric, red chilli powder, and salt.
2. Wet your hands and gently knead the spices into the meat.
3. Add the peanut oil and water to help work the spice mixture in. Knead again. Cover the bowl and leave for 2 hours.
4. To make the sauce, combine the desiccated coconut and water. Mix well. Strain the mixture through a fine sieve, pressing the coconut milk into a bowl with a wooden spoon.
5. Grind the peanuts coarsely.
6. Add the turmeric, curry powder, red chilli powder, and sugar to the coconut milk.
7. Cook the coconut milk mixture over medium heat, stirring, until the sauce comes to the boil.
8. Reduce the heat to low and add the ground peanuts. Continue to cook, stirring constantly, for 2 minutes.

Method

9. Add the lemon juice and salt to taste.
10. Remove the sauce from the heat and cool.
11. Preheat the grill.
12. Thread 8 thin metal or bamboo skewers with 4 pieces of chicken each. The skewer enters the meat 2–3 times, like a needle threading through cloth.
13. Brush the chicken satays with peanut oil and grill for 10–14 minutes, turning frequently, until the satays are cooked through (about 4–6 minutes on each side).
14. Serve hot with the peanut sauce.

N.B : If a grill is not available, the skewers can be grilled in a non-stick pan on a slow-flame.

Ingredients

Peanut sauce

100 gms desiccated coconut
300 ml water
100 gms salted peanuts
½ tsp turmeric powder
½ tsp curry powder
¼ tsp red chilli powder
2 tbsp sugar
1 tsp lemon juice

Fried Wontons

Ingredients

- 450 gms chicken mince
- 8 shrimps, shelled and deveined
- 8 water chestnuts*
- 1 spring onion
- 1 tsp oil
- A pinch of MSG (optional)
- 8 Wonton wrappers
- Oil for frying

Sauce

- 1 cup pineapple juice
- ¼ cup vinegar
- 1 cup brown sugar
- ½ cup tomato paste
- Salt to taste

*Can be subsitituted with carrots

Method

1. Mince the shrimp, water chestnuts and spring onion.
2. Add the chicken mince.
3. Stir in the oil and MSG.
4. Place a teaspoon of the mixture on a wonton wrapper.
5. Dip your finger in water and moisten the edges of the wrapper.
6. Gather up the edges together over the filling, to make a small bundle, and press lightly to seal.
7. Repeat for the rest of the wrappers.
8. Heat the oil and deep fry the prepared wontons.
9. To make the sauce, mix all the ingredients together and cook over low heat, stirring to dissolve sugar.
10. Simmer for 5 minutes. Let cool.
11. Serve the hot wontons with the sauce for dipping.

Eggplant Dip

Method

1. Cook the eggplant directly on the gas flame, turning frequently, until completely tender inside and charred on the outside.
2. Peel off and discard the charred outer skin carefully.
3. Place the eggplant meat in a bowl and mash with a fork.
4. Add the olive oil, a little at a time, working it in continuously with the fork.
5. Add the lemon juice, a little at a time, and mix.
6. Mix in the garlic, salt and pepper, mashing everything together until well blended.
7. Chill for about 30 minutes.
8. Let stand for a further 30 minutes to reach room temperature.
9. Serve with feta cheese, cold cuts and breadsticks.

Ingredients

1 round eggplant
½ cup olive oil
Juice of 1 lemon
1 clove garlic, crushed
Salt and pepper to taste
Feta cheese, cold cuts and breadsticks, to serve

Hummus

Ingredients

- 250 gms chickpeas
- Salt to taste
- 1¾ tbsp sesame seeds
- ½ cup olive oil
- 1¾ tbsp garlic paste
- 3 tbsp lemon juice
- Red chilli powder, chopped fresh coriander leaves for garnishing

Method

1. Soak the chickpeas overnight.
2. Wash with several changes of water. Pressure cook with a little salt and plenty of water until soft. Drain and save the cooking liquid.
3. Grind the sesame seeds with a little olive oil.
4. While still warm, put the chickpeas into grinder with 2–3 tablespoon of the cooking liquid, garlic paste, sesame seeds paste, and lemon juice. If the puree looks coarse add a little more of the cooking liquid. The puree should look like baby food.
5. Towards the end of grinding, add the olive oil and whisk once.
6. Transfer to a shallow bowl. Make a dent in the centre of the hummus with the back of a spoon. Pour 100 ml of olive oil into the cavity.
7. Sprinkle some red chilli powder and fresh coriander leaves on top.
8. Serve chilled, as a spread or with bread and/or fresh vegetable slices.

Pâté Maison

Method

1. Preheat the oven to 170°C.
2. Line a 5 inch x 7 inch tin with the bacon rashers.
3. Mince both kinds of livers.
4. Add the garlic, egg, cream, brandy, salt and pepper.
5. Mix well and transfer to the tin.
6. Cover with a foil and put the tin in a dish with water coming half way up the sides.
7. Bake in the hot oven for about 2 hours.
8. Cool and chill overnight. Turn out of the mould just before serving.
9. Slice and serve with bread or toast, lettuce and/or tomatoes.

Ingredients

150 gms bacon rashers
600 gms lamb liver
200 gms chicken liver
1 clove garlic, crushed
1 egg, beaten
2 tbsp cream
2 tsp brandy
Salt and pepper to taste

Tempura

Ingredients

- 2 carrots, finely sliced
- 2 capsicums, sliced
- 18 green beans, sliced
- 12 large prawns, par-boiled
- 1 egg
- 200 gms flour
- 4 tbsp ice-cold water
- 3 cubes of ice
- Salt to taste
- 4 tbsp dry sherry
- 4 tbsp soy sauce
- 2 tbsp wasabi or mustard paste
- 4 cups oil for frying

Method

1. Mix the egg, flour, water, and ice. Blend well to get a smooth liquid batter. Add salt.
2. Heat the oil until it is very hot.
3. Dip the vegetables and the prawns into the batter and deep fry.
4. To make the dip, mix together the sherry, the soy sauce and the wasabi.
5. Serve the tempura hot with the dip.

Sushi Rice

Method

1. Wash the rice and let it drain for an hour before cooking.
2. Put the rice and water in a heavy saucepan and bring to a boil. Cover, reduce heat and let it simmer for 15–20 minutes. The rice for sushi is a little harder than you would normally cook it. Remove from heat and leave it covered for 10 minutes.
3. Mix together the vinegar, salt and sugar and bring to a boil. As soon as it starts boiling, remove from fire.
4. Pour the vinegar sauce over the rice.
5. Mix gently, taking care not to break the rice kernels. Leave to cool.
6. Shape about 2 tablespoons of the sushi rice into a finger of about 1-inch by 2-inch. Repeat with the rest of the rice.
7. Serve at room temperature.

Ingredients

- 3 cups long-grain rice
- 3½ cups water
- 3 tbsp vinegar
- 4½ tbsp sugar
- 2 tsp salt

Herb and Tomato Salsa

Ingredients

450 gms tomatoes, seeded and diced
1 small onion, chopped
8 basil leaves, roughly chopped
2 tbsp chopped fresh parsley
1 garlic clove, crushed
4 tsp olive oil
1 tbsp balsamic vinegar
A dash of Tabasco and worcestershire sauce
Salt and black pepper
Taco chips, to serve

Method

1. Place all the ingredients in a non-metallic bowl and stir until well combined.
2. Serve with taco chips.

Oriental Fried Shrimps

Method

1. Wash the shrimps and boil them in a covered, shallow pan. Add about 1 teaspoon of salt to the water while boiling.
2. Stir and remove as soon as the shells turn red.
3. Shell and de-vein the shrimps, but leave the tail.
4. Beat the egg white until soft peaks form then beat in the egg yolk.
5. Add the salt, baking powder and flour. Beat for about another minute.
6. Heat the oil until smoking hot.
7. Holding each shrimp by its tail, dip it in the batter and fry until golden brown. Drain on paper towels.
8. Serve hot with ketchup or sweet and sour sauce.

Ingredients

250 gms medium-sized shrimps
1 egg, separated
1½ tsp salt
½ tsp baking powder
3 tbsp flour
Oil for frying
Ketchup or sweet and sour sauce, to serve

Soups

Chicken Soup with Meatballs

Method

1. Combine the meatball ingredients and shape them into balls, about ¾ inch in diameter.
2. Bring the stock to a boil. Add the remaining soup ingredients and the meatballs to the stock.
3. Cook over medium heat until vegetables are tender and meatballs are cooked through.
4. Serve hot.

Ingredients

- 8 cups chicken stock
- ¾ cup chopped cauliflower florets
- 1 cup chopped broccoli florets
- 1 cup chopped squash (a mixture of acorn, zucchini and summer squash)
- 3 carrots, sliced 4 spring onions, chopped
- Salt to taste
- 1 tbsp chopped mixed fresh herbs (parsley and coriander)

Meatballs

- 225 gms chicken mince
- ⅛ cup bread crumbs
- ¼ tsp nutmeg
- ¼ tsp salt
- Pepper to taste

Egg and Lemon Soup

Ingredients

- 6 cups chicken stock
- 2 tbsp soup pasta or rice
- 3 eggs
- Juice of 1 lemon
- 1 tbsp cold water
- Salt and pepper to taste

Method

1. Bring the stock to a boil and add the pasta. Let it cook till the pasta is nearly cooked.
2. Beat the eggs in a large bowl until they become a little frothy (a little more than you beat them for scrambled eggs). Add the lemon juice and water. Stir well.
3. Take a ladleful of the hot stock and add it very slowly to the egg and lemon mixture, stirring as you go. If the broth goes in too fast, the eggs will curdle.
4. Take the stock away from the heat. Now pour the egg mixture into the remainder of the broth.
5. Season with salt and pepper.
6. Stir and serve.

Country-style Gazpacho

Method

1. Combine all the ingredients.
2. Chill well, for about 4 hours.
3. Garnish with croutons and serve.

Ingredients

1 cup chopped tomato
½ cup chopped capsicum
½ cup chopped celery
½ cup chopped cucumber
¼ cup chopped onion
2 tsp chopped parsley
1 clove garlic, minced
2–3 tbsp wine vinegar
2 tbsp olive oil
1 tsp salt
¼ tsp pepper
½ tsp Worcestershire sauce
2 cups tomato juice
Croutons for garnishing

Chicken and Asparagus Soup

Ingredients

- 500 gms chicken breast, cut into small pieces
- 2 tsp salt
- 2 tbsp dry sherry
- 2 tbsp cornflour
- 6 cups chicken stock
- 2 tsp soy sauce
- 250 gms asparagus, chopped
- ½ lemon

Method

1. Marinate the chicken pieces in salt and sherry for 30 minutes.
2. Drain the chicken pieces and retain the juices.
3. Dust the chicken pieces with cornflour and poach in boiling water till they are cooked, about 10 minutes.
4. Heat the chicken stock in a saucepan and bring to simmer.
5. Add the drained juices (step 2), soy sauce and asparagus and let it simmer for another 5 minutes.
6. Place some asparagus and some chicken in individual bowls and pour in enough of the boiling stock to fill the bowl.
7. Serve hot.

Sotsuppe (Fruit Soup)

Method

1. Combine all the ingredients except the arrowroot and raspberries in a large saucepan.
2. Simmer for 1 hour.
3. Sprinkle the arrowroot over the soup and stir to avoid lumping. Cook for 15 minutes more.
4. Add the raspberries and stir occasionally. Cook for 2–3 minutes.
5. Serve either warm or chilled.

Ingredients

- 1 cup pitted prunes
- 1 cup raisins
- 1 cup peeled, chopped apple
- 1 tbsp finely chopped orange peel
- 1 orange, peeled and cut
- 4 cups water
- 1 tbsp lemon juice
- ¼ cup sugar
- 1 stick cinnamon
- ¼ tsp salt
- 2 tbsp arrowroot
- 280 gms raspberries

Yayla Corbasi (Yoghurt Rice Soup)

Ingredients

6	cups chicken stock
½	cup rice
1	tbsp flour
2	cups yoghurt
1	egg
1	tbsp finely chopped mint

Method

1. Mix the rice and the stock. Cook the soup till the rice is almost done.
2. In another bowl, mix the flour, egg and yoghurt.
3. Beat about ¼ cup of the simmering soup into this mixture. Add another ½ cup and mix.
4. Pour the mixture back into the cooking soup stirring constantly.
5. Simmer until the soup is thick enough.
6. Stir in the mint just before serving.

Spicy Tomato Rasam

Method

1. Blanch the tomatoes in boiling water. Peel and grate.
2. Heat ¼ teaspoon of the oil. Add the pepper corns and 1 teaspoon of cumin seeds.
3. Roast till aromatic, then grind till powdered. Keep aside.
4. Combine the tomato pulp, whole chillies, curry leaves, mint, fresh coriander, clove-cinnamon powder, *sambhar masala*, tamarind, jaggery, peppercorn, and cumin powder. Mash well to blend.
5. Add the boiled-gram water.
6. Heat the remaining oil in a small pan, add the mustard, the remaining cumin seeds and asafoetida and allow to splutter.
7. Add the garlic and stir, add carefully to the rasam.
8. Bring the rasam to a boil. Check spices and salt and adjust. Simmer for 2–3 minutes.
9. Keep aside covered for 10 minutes before serving.

Ingredients

2 large tomatoes
4 cups liqueur of boiled gram (after it has boiled for 30 minutes or till it is cooked)
2 whole red chillies, dry roasted
1 sprig curry leaves
1 sprig mint leaves
1 sprig fresh coriander leaves
2–3 pinches of clove-cinnamon powder
½ tsp *sambar masala*
1 marble-sized ball of jaggery or ½ tsp sugar
1 small strip tamarind
8-10 peppercorns
1½ tsp cumin seeds
½ tsp mustard seeds
2 pinches of asafoetida
1–2 garlic clove, grated
1 tbsp oil
Salt to taste

Bouillabaise

Ingredients

1 kg mixed fish (at least two different types of fish), cut into thick pieces
3 onions, sliced
1 stick celery, chopped
¾ cup olive oil
250 gms tomatoes, skinned and sliced
2 cloves garlic, crushed
1 bay leaf
A few sprigs of parsley
A pinch of dried thyme and fennel (optional)
Finely shredded rind of ½ orange
Salt and pepper to taste
A pinch of saffron
A pinch of cinnamon powder
4 Bread slices to serve

Method

1. Sauté the onions and celery in oil till soft.
2. Stir in the tomatoes, garlic, herbs, orange rind, and seasoning.
3. Place all the firmer-fleshed fish in a layer over the vegetables.
4. Cover with water in which saffron has been steeped.
5. Boil for about 8 minutes before adding the softer fish.
6. Continue cooking till all the ingredients are cooked but still in shape.
7. Pour into individual bowls containing a slice of bread each to serve.

Velours d'Aubergine

Ingredients

- 4 tbsp butter
- 1 cup chopped onion
- ½ cup chopped celery
- 1 large aubergine, peeled and cubed
- 4 cups chicken stock
- 1 tsp curry powder
- ½ tsp dried basil
- A pinch of thyme
- Salt, pepper and cayenne to taste
- 1 large potato, thinly sliced
- 2 tbsp cream
- ½ tsp Worcestershire sauce

Method

1. Melt the butter. Add the chopped onions and celery. Cook slowly till the vegetables are tender. Do not brown.
2. Add the aubergine to the pot. Cook for about 5 minutes, stirring often.
3. Add the stock and seasonings. Simmer uncovered for 15 minutes.
4. Add the potato and cook until tender.
5. Blend and put through a strainer to remove all the seeds. Let cool completely.
6. Add the cream and Worcestershire sauce and serve cold.

Peanut Butter Chowder

Ingredients

- ¼ cup butter
- ½ cup julienned carrots
- ½ cup julienned zucchini
- ½ cup julienned red or green capsicum
- ½ cup shredded red cabbage
- ½ cup chopped onion
- 8 tbsp flour
- 5 cups chicken stock
- 1 cup creamy peanut butter
- 1 cup light cream or milk
- ½ tsp salt
- ¼ tsp pepper
- Chopped salted peanuts for garnishing

Method

1. Melt the butter. Add the vegetables and sauté for 3 minutes.
2. Add the flour and stir till well mixed and smooth.
3. Stir in the stock and bring to a boil.
4. Stir in the peanut butter; reduce the heat and simmer for 15 minutes. Remove from heat.
5. Stir in the cream, salt and pepper.
6. Garnish with peanuts and serve.

Salads

Asparagi Pietro

Method

1. Choose the thin spears of asparagus. Trim off the tough ends and peel the lower half of the stalks.
2. Steam the asparagus; do not overcook.
3. Beat together the vinegar, salt, pepper, and oil.
4. Stir in the eggs and the spring onions. Spoon over the asparagus.
5. Chill and serve.

Ingredients

- 1½ kg asparagus
- 3 tbsp red wine vinegar
- 1 tsp salt
- ½ tsp freshly ground black pepper
- ¾ cup olive oil
- 3 hard-boiled eggs, chopped
- 5 spring onions, sliced

Avocado Salad

Ingredients

6 large avocados, diced
2 fresh tomatoes, diced
¼ onion, diced
8 radishes, diced
100 gms fresh coriander leaves, finely chopped
Salt to taste

Method

1. Mix all the ingredients, except salt, in a large bowl. Remember to leave the avocado pits in the salad so that the avocado does not turn brown.
2. Remove the pits and add salt just before serving.

Chicken Salad

Ingredients

- 3 chicken breast halves
- Salt and pepper to taste
- 225 gms Chinese rice noodles
- 1 small head lettuce, torn into bite-sized pieces
- 4 spring onions, thinly slivered
- 2 tbsp sesame seeds, toasted
- 2 tbsp almonds, slivered

Dressing

- 2 tbsp sugar
- 1 tsp salt
- 1 tsp MSG (optional)
- ½ tsp cracked pepper
- ¼ cup peanut oil
- 1 tbsp sesame oil
- 3 tbsp vinegar

Method

1. Season the chicken with salt and pepper.
2. Bake or broil till tender. Cut into thin slices.
3. Deep fry the Chinese rice noodles.
4. Mix the ingredients for dressing.
5. Toss the lettuce and chicken with the dressing.
6. Just before serving, add the fried noodles to the chicken and toss.
7. Place the salad on a platter and garnish with the spring onions, sesame seeds and almonds before serving.

Angourosalata me Yiaourti
(Cucumbers and Yoghurt Salad)

Ingredients

- 2 large cucumbers, diced
- 250 gms yoghurt
- ¼ cup sliced spring onion
- 1 tbsp finely chopped fresh mint
- 2 cloves garlic, minced
- 1 tbsp vinegar
- ½ tsp salt
- ¼ tsp pepper
- Fresh mint for garnishing

Method

1. Combine all the ingredients.
2. Refrigerate for at least 1 hour for the flavour to develop.
3. Garnish with additional fresh mint before serving.

Potato Salad

Method

1. Cook the bacon and onion in a frying pan until brown and crisp.
2. Cool and mix in the mayonnaise, vinegar, sugar, salt, and pepper.
3. Add the potatoes.
4. Preheat the oven to 180°C.
5. Transfer to a baking dish and bake for approximately 30 minutes.
6. Serve warm.

Ingredients

- 4-5 slices bacon, cut into small pieces
- ½ cup chopped onion
- ½ cup mayonnaise
- 2 tbsp cider vinegar
- ¼ cup sugar
- Salt and pepper to taste
- 4 cups boiled and sliced potatoes

Orange and Onion Salad

Ingredients

½ tsp sugar
1 onion, sliced thin
4 oranges, peeled and sliced
5-6 pitted black olives, sliced
French dressing
Lettuce leaves

Method

1. Sprinkle the onions with sugar and let sweat for 15 minutes.
2. To assemble, place the sliced oranges on a bed of lettuce.
3. Push the drained onions into rings and place them on top of the oranges.
4. Top with the sliced black olives.
5. Cover with a simple French dressing.

Tri-coloured Salad with Vinaigrette

Method

1. Place all the dressing ingredients in a jar. Screw on the lid and shake well.
2. Blanch the French beans.
3. Place the vegetables in separate bowls.
4. Pour ⅓ of the dressing over each vegetable. Toss to combine.
5. Check seasoning.
6. Serve on platter in separate mounds.

Ingredients

Dressing

- 2 tbsp wine vinegar
- 6 tbsp olive oil
- ¼ tsp salt
- ⅛ tsp ground pepper
- ¼ tsp mustard
- 1 tbsp chopped fresh parsley, chervil, chives, basil, tarragon, or thyme (or 1 tsp dried herbs)
- 450 gms French beans, cut diagonally
- 4 large carrots, peeled and shredded
- 4 small beetroots, peeled and shredded

Wilted Lettuce

Ingredients

- 8 cups lettuce
- 3 bacon slices, cut into pieces
- 1 tbsp flour
- 2 tbsp sugar
- 1 egg, beaten
- ¼ cup vinegar
- 1 cup water
- 2 tbsp mustard paste
- Hard-boiled eggs (optional)

Method

1. Wash and dry the lettuce and tear into bite-sized pieces.
2. Fry the bacon until crisp and remove from drippings.
3. Mix together the flour and the sugar.
4. Add the remaining ingredients to this.
   Stir until well blended.
5. Add the mixture to the bacon drippings and cook until thickened.
6. Pour the hot dressing over the lettuce.
7. Garnish with bacon pieces and, if desired, sliced hard-boiled eggs.

Russian Salad

Method

1. For the white sauce, heat the butter in a pan.
2. Add the flour, and keep stirring continuously so that it does not form lumps.
3. Add the milk while stirring. Remove from heat when the sauce begins to thicken.
4. Allow the sauce to cool a little and then add the salt, sugar and black pepper powder followed by the potatoes, carrot and pineapple.
5. Refrigrate the salad.
6. Mix the Mayonnaise before serving.
7. Garnish with fresh cherries and boiled eggs and serve.

Ingredients

- 1 cup boiled & cubed potatoes
- ½ cup cubed & blanched carrot
- ½ cup sliced pineapple
- Salt to taste
- ½ tsp sugar
- ¼ tsp black pepper powder

For the white sauce

- 2 tsp butter
- 2 tsp flour
- 2 cups milk
- Fresh cherries for garnishing
- ½ cup Mayonnaise
- 2 boiled eggs quartered length-wise

Chicken and Fruit Salad

Ingredients

- 175 gms boneless chicken breasts, cut into long thin strips
- 125 gms peeled prawns, chopped
- 5 cloves garlic, peeled and cut into slivers
- 100 gms spring onions, halved and thinly sliced
- 1¼ tsp salt
- 1 tsp caster sugar
- 3 tbsp limejuice
- 1 red chilli, deseeded and thinly sliced
- 1 green chilli, deseeded and thinly sliced
- 1 large cooking apple, peeled, cored and diced
- 150 gms seedless black grapes, sliced

Method

1. Place the diced apples in a bowl and cover with salted water until ready to use.
2. Heat the oil. Fry the garlic slivers until golden. Drain.
3. Add the spring onions to the hot oil. Stir-fry until golden. Drain. Reserve a portion for garnishing.
4. Place the chicken in another pan. Add water to cover and add ¼ teaspoon of salt to it.
5. Bring to a simmer and cook gently for 3–4 minutes or until the chicken is just about done. Add the prawns and cook for another minute.
6. Remove the chicken and prawns.
7. Separate the chicken. Tear it into shreds. Combine the prawns and the chicken. Set aside.
8. In a bowl, combine 1 teaspoon each of salt and sugar with the limejuice, whisk well and set aside.

Method

9. Drain the apples and pat them dry.
10. Toss all the ingredients together in a bowl. Pour the lime juice mixture over the salad and season with salt and pepper to taste.
11. Serve on individual plates and garnish with the spring onions and coriander leaves.

Ingredients

- 150 gms seedless green grapes, sliced
- 1 orange, peeled and roughly chopped
- 4 tbsp peanuts, lightly crushed
- 2 tbsp fresh coriander leaves
- Salt and pepper to taste
- Oil for frying
- Chopped spring onions and fresh coriander leaves for garnishing

Vegetables

Bean Sprouts with Mushrooms and Garlic

Method

1. Heat the oil in a wok. Add the garlic, mushrooms and spring onions.
2. Stir-fry for a minute before adding the bean sprouts. Mix thoroughly.
3. Add the remaining ingredients and stir-fry until the mixture boils and thickens.
4. Serve hot.

Ingredients

1 clove garlic, thinly sliced
8 mushrooms, finely chopped
4 spring onions, sliced diagonally
250 gms bean sprouts
2 tsp oil
1 tbsp oyster sauce
2 tsp soy sauce
1 tbsp dry sherry
2 tsp cornflour
3 tbsp water

Szechwan Eggplant (Brinjal)

Ingredients

500 gms long eggplant
1 tbsp soy sauce
1 tbsp sugar
60 ml vegetable stock
5 tbsp peanut oil
2 tsp freshly grated ginger
3 cloves garlic, crushed
¼ tsp dried chilli flakes
100 gms water chestnuts, chopped*
3 spring onions, chopped
1 tbsp red wine vinegar
1 tbsp sesame oil
1 tbsp sesame seeds, toasted, to garnish

*Can be substituted with blanched, peeled and halved (*length-wise, along the natural break*) almonds

Method

1. Cut the aubergine into half inch by 2 inch strips.
2. Mix together the soy sauce, sugar and stock. Set aside.
3. Heat 2 tablespoons of the peanut oil until very hot and almost smoking.
4. Add half of the aubergine and stir-fry for 4–5 minutes. Remove from the pan and set aside.
5. Add another 2 tablespoons of peanut oil to the pan, reheat until very hot then stir-fry the remaining uncooked aubergine for 4–5 minutes. Remove from the pan and set aside.
6. Add the remaining tablespoon of the peanut oil and heat until hot. Add the ginger, garlic and chilli flakes. Sauté gently until softened.
7. Add the water chestnuts and half of the spring onions. Stir-fry for 30 seconds.

Method

8. Increase heat to high. Add the soy sauce mixture and the cooked aubergine.
9. Toss quickly over high heat for 1–2 minutes until the sauce has reduced and been absorbed by the aubergine.
10. Stir in the vinegar and the sesame oil and mix well.
11. Serve garnished with the remaining chopped spring onions and sesame seeds.

Marinated Mushrooms

Ingredients

36	button mushrooms, stems removed
1	onion, minced finely
2	tbsp soy sauce
4	tbsp wine vinegar
3	tbsp dry sherry
2	tbsp sugar
1	tsp salt

Method

1. Mix together the onion, soy sauce, vinegar, sherry, sugar, and salt in a saucepan.
2. Bring to a boil. Let it boil for a minute.
3. Pour the boiling marinade over the mushrooms.
4. Let the marinated mushrooms stand in the refrigerator overnight.
5. Drain and serve.

Chiles Rellenos

Method

1. Preheat the oven to 180°C.
2. Cut the tops from the peppers and scoop out the pith and the seeds.
3. Chop the pepper tops.
4. Heat the oil in a saucepan. Add the onions, red chillies and chopped pepper tops.
5. Fry until softened.
6. Stir in the cottage cheese, oregano and Tabasco. Fry for 5–6 minutes.
7. Add the flour, stock, tomato paste, salt and pepper.
8. Cover and simmer for 30 minutes, stirring occasionally.
9. Stuff the peppers with the above prepared mixture.
10. Arrange in a greased baking dish and bake for 40 minutes.
11. To make the sauce, combine the cream cheese, cream, and red chilli powder in a saucepan.

Ingredients

- 4 large green or red chilli peppers
- ¼ cup olive oil
- 2 onions, finely chopped
- 2 dried red chillies, crumbled
- 450 gms freshly made cottage cheese, crumbled
- 1 tsp dried oregano
- ½ tsp Tabasco sauce
- 2 tbsp flour
- 1 cup vegetable stock
- 3 tbsp tomato paste
- Salt and pepper to taste

Sauce

- 225 gms cream cheese
- ½ cup light cream
- ¼ tsp red chilli powder
- ½ cup raisins

Method

12. Heat gently, stirring until the mixture is smooth and hot.
13. Stir in the raisins.
14. Pour the sauce over the peppers and bake for a further 15 minutes.
15. Serve when ready.

Gado Gado

Method

1. Parboil the carrots and French beans. Drain and set aside.
2. Blanch the cabbage.
3. Heat oil. Fry the red chillies for 3–4 minutes, then remove and drain.
4. Fry the garlic in the same way.
5. Grind together the fried garlic and chillies.
6. Add the peanut butter and the coconut milk to the paste. Blend together.
7. Pour into a saucepan and add the lemon juice. Bring to boil and allow the sauce to thicken but still retain its pouring consistency.
8. Mix together the bean sprouts, cucumber, French beans, cabbage, potatoes, and carrots in a large serving bowl.
9. Pour over the cooled peanut sauce and garnish with celery, spring onions and eggs to serve.

Ingredients

- 2 carrots, peeled and cut into thin strips
- 250 gms French beans, cut diagonally
- ½ small cabbage, shredded
- 2 cups bean sprouts
- 1 small cucumber, chopped
- 3 potatoes, boiled and sliced
- 2 tbsp oil
- 4 fresh red chillies
- 3 cloves garlic
- 250 gms crunchy peanut butter
- 4 cups coconut milk
- 2 tsp lemon juice
- 2 stalks celery, finely chopped
- 3 spring onions, chopped
- 3 hardboiled eggs, shelled and quartered

Rotkohimit Apfein (Red Cabbage with Apples)

Ingredients

900 gms red cabbage*, shredded finely
⅔ cup red wine vinegar
2 tbsp sugar
2 tsp salt
2 tbsp butter
2 medium apples, peeled, cored and thinly sliced
½ cup chopped onion
1 onion, peeled and studded with 6 cloves
1 bay leaf
1 cup boiling water
3 tbsp red wine**
4 tbsp red currant jelly***

*Can be substituted with green cabbage mixed with beetroot juice

**Balsamic vinagar can be used instead

***Grape jam/conserve is a close substitute

Method

1. Toss the cabbage in a bowl with the wine vinegar, sugar and salt. Let rest for a few minutes.
2. Melt the butter. Sauté the apples and the chopped onion.
3. When the onions are soft and the apples lightly browned, add the cabbage with all of the liquid from the bowl.
4. Add the whole onion, bay leaf and boiling water.
5. Bring to a boil, then reduce heat and simmer for about 2 hours, covered. If cabbage looks too wet, uncover the pot for a while.
6. Before serving, remove the whole onion and the bay leaf and stir in the wine and jelly.

Stir-fried Tofu with Vegetables

Method

1. Heat the oil for frying. Lightly fry the tofu.
2. Heat 3 tablespoons of oil in a wok. Stir-fry the onions and garlic.
3. Add the tofu and vegetables. Stir-fry until the vegetables are tender but crisp.
4. Season with soy sauce, salt and pepper.
5. Serve with rice.

Ingredients

450 gms tofu, cut into cubes
¼ cup chopped onions
3 cloves garlic, minced
1 green capsicum, chopped
1 red capsicum, chopped
1 cup carrots, sliced
1 cup shredded cabbage
½ cup cauliflower florets
½ cup broccoli florets
2 tbsp soy sauce
Salt and pepper to taste
Oil for frying
Rice to serve

Stuffed Avocados

Ingredients

- 4 avocados
- 400 gms boiled, mixed vegetables (carrots, peas, cauliflower, beans)
- 1 large potato, cooked and cut into small squares
- 3-4 tbsp mayonnaise
- 1 tbsp lemon juice
- 1 tomato, sliced

Method

1. Cut each avocado in half. Empty each avocado half with a tablespoon and cut the emptied inside into squares.
2. Mix the vegetables, avocado cubes and mayonnaise. Reserve the mixture.
3. Sprinkle the lemon juice in each avocado shell.
4. Fill each avocado half with the prepared mixture and decorate with one slice of tomato before serving.

Kugelis (Potato Casserole)

Method

1. Peel the potatoes and cover with cold water for half and hour.
2. Preheat the oven to 200°C.
3. Oil a deep casserole.
4. Grate the potatoes to a medium-fine consistency. As you grate, let the potatoes drain in a mesh colander. When the colander is full, transfer the potatoes to the baking dish.
5. Fry the bacon in a covered frying pan until crisp, stirring as often as needed.
6. Drain off any excess liquid from the potatoes.
7. Stir in the bacon, with the bacon grease and the salt.
8. Beat the eggs and stir into the potato mixture.
9. Mix in the milk and milk powder.

Ingredients

2¼ kg new red potatoes*

450 gms bacon, cut in small pieces

1 tbsp salt

6 eggs

400 gms milk powder

2 cups milk

*You can use the regular new potatoes too

Method

10. Bake for 30 minutes at 200°C, then at 180°C for another 30 minutes. A knife inserted in the centre of the kugelis should come out pretty clean.
11. Let stand for 15 minutes before serving; it shouldn't be too hot.
12. Cut into squares and serve with sour cream.

Pierogi

Method

1. For the filling, boil the potatoes until soft. Drain and mash them.
2. Beat in the cheese, butter, salt and pepper.
3. Mound the flour in a bowl and make a well in the centre.
4. Place the eggs and salt in the well and add water.
5. Gradually mix the wet ingredients into the dry. Knead the dough until firm and well mixed. Cover the dough with a warmed bowl and let rest for 15 minutes.
6. Divide the dough in half. Roll one portion out thin.
7. Cut into rounds with a large biscuit cutter.
8. Place a spoonful of filling a little off the centre on each round. Moisten the edges of the round with a little water.

Ingredients

- 2 cups flour
- 2 eggs
- ½ tsp salt
- ⅓ cup water

Potato and cheese filling

- 4 potatoes, peeled and diced
- 1 cup grated cheese
- 1 tbsp butter
- Salt and pepper

For frying

- 3 tbsp butter
- 1 cup chopped onions

Method

9. Fold the dough over the filling and press the edges together firmly. Be sure that they are well sealed to prevent the filling from running out while the pierogi are cooking. Repeat with the rest of the dough and the filling.
10. Bring water to a boil in a large saucepan. Drop the pierogi into the boiling water. Do not overcrowd the pan. Cook for 3 to 5 minutes. Lift out with a perforated spoon.
11. In heavy pan melt the butter and the add onions. Fry till the onions become transparent. Add the pierogi and fry golden.
12. Serve hot with onion.

Celery Bake

Method

1. Preheat the oven to 180°C.
2. Toss the breadcrumbs with 2 tablespoons of butter and set aside.
3. Heat the remaining butter. Cook the celery in it until tender.
4. Add the flour and salt. Stir until the flour is absorbed.
5. Stir in the milk gradually.
6. Add the mushrooms, capsicum, pimento, onion, and parsley.
7. Add the cheese.
8. Turn into a baking dish.
9. Top with breadcrumbs.
10. Bake for 30 minutes.

Ingredients

2 cups fresh breadcrumbs
4 tbsp butter, melted
4 cups sliced celery
3 tbsp flour
1 tsp salt
1 cup milk
85 gms mushrooms
2 tbsp chopped capsicum
2 tbsp pimento*
2 tbsp minced onions
1 tbsp parsley
110 gms sharp cheese, grated**

*If not available, use red pepper

**Strong cheddar, Blue Stilten or Strong Gouda

Sweet and Sour Vegetables

Ingredients

- 2¼ tsp vinegar
- ¾ cup sugar
- ¼ cup brown sugar
- ¼ cup water
- 2 tsp soy sauce
- ¾ tsp ginger
- A dash of tabasco and worcestershire sauce
- 2 tbsp pineapple juice
- 2 tbsp ketchup (tomato sauce)
- 3 tbsp cornflour
- ½ cup pineapple chunks
- 4 cups boiled, mixed vegetables (carrots, peas, cauliflower, beans)

Method

1. Combine all the ingredients except corn flour, pineapple and mixed vegetables in a saucepan.
2. Cook and simmer till the sauce thickens. Add the corn flour mixed with a little cold water.
3. Add the pineapple chunks and heat through.
4. Add the vegetables and cook for 4–5 minutes.
5. Serve hot.

Masala Stuffed Mirchi (Stuffed Chilli Fritters)

Method

1. Slit the chillies lengthwise and de-seed.
2. Mix all the spices and stuff the chillies with the mixture.
3. Mix the gram flour with a little salt and red chilli powder. Add a small quantity of water to make a thick paste.
4. Dip each chilli into this mixture to coat.
5. Heat the oil in a wok and shallow fry the chillies, a few at a time.
6. Place the fried chillies in a pan and sprinkle with a little water. Cover the pan and allow to cook for a few minutes.
7. Serve hot.

Ingredients

10 large green chillies
1½ tsp coriander powder
1½ tsp cumin powder
½ tsp turmeric powder
½ tsp carom seeds
½ tsp red chilli powder
Salt to taste
1¼ cup gram flour
¼ cup oil

Mashed Potatoes

Ingredients

4	large potatoes
1	cup milk or sour cream
¼	cup butter
	Salt and pepper to taste

Method

1. Peel the potatoes and cut into quarters.
2. Place in a large saucepan with enough water to cover. Bring to a boil, lower the heat and cook for about 25–30 minutes, or until tender. Drain well.
3. Place the potatoes in the mixing bowl of an electric mixer and beat until smooth.
4. Heat the milk or cream in a small saucepan and add to the potatoes along with butter, salt and pepper.
5. Beat until smooth and fluffy.
6. Serve hot.

Vegetable Stroganoff

Method

1. Melt 3 tablespoons of butter in a pan. Add the onions and mushrooms and sauté until the onions are soft.
2. Add the sour cream, yoghurt, wine, salt, dill-weed, tamari, red chilli, black pepper, and the remaining butter. Mix well.
3. Transfer the mixture to the top of a double boiler and simmer over hot water for 30 minutes, stirring often.
4. Steam the chopped vegetables until tender.
5. Cook the noodles in boiling salted water until tender. Drain.
6. Place the noodles and vegetables in a large serving dish. Pour the sauce over the noodles and vegetables and mix gently. Garnish with the minced spring onions before serving.

Ingredients

5 tbsp butter
1 cup chopped onions
225 gms mushrooms, chopped
3 cups sour cream*
1½ cups yoghurt
3 tbsp dry red wine
¾ tsp salt
¼ tsp dried dill-weed (optional)
Dash of soy sauce
Red chilli powder-to taste
Ground black pepper-to taste
6 cups chopped mixed vegetables (broccoli, cauliflower, capsicum, carrots, cherry tomatoes)
4 cups uncooked wide egg noodles
1 bunch spring onions, minced

*Can be substituted with muslin hung yoghurt

Curried Stuffed Eggplant

Ingredients

2½ kg small, round eggplants
50 gms roasted peanuts
2 tsp red chilli powder
1 tsp turmeric powder
1 tsp *garam masala*
10 gms jaggery
20 gms tamarind
1 tsp mustard seeds
½ tsp asafoetida
Salt to taste
Oil
Fresh coriander leaves and grated coconut for garnishing

Method

1. Soak the tamarind in half cup of water for 15 minutes. Extract the juice. Set aside.
2. Mix all the ingredients except the tamarind, jaggery, mustard seeds, and asafoetida.
3. Cut a slit in each of the eggplants. Stuff the spice mixture into the slits.
4. Heat the oil. Add the mustard seeds and asafoetida.
5. Add the stuffed eggplants.
6. Cover and cook for 5 minutes.
7. Add the tamarind extract and jaggery. Cover and cook until the eggplants are done.
8. Garnish with fresh coriander and grated coconut.
9. Serve hot.

Cauliflower Tikka

Method

1. Wash the cauliflowers in salted water and cut into 2-inch pieces.
2. Mix all the spices. Add the cauliflower. Marinate for a couple of hours.
3. Brush the cauliflower pieces lightly with oil. Put about six pieces on each skewer and grill over charcoal fire.
4. Keep turning the skewers around till well done.
5. Sprinkle *chaat masala* and serve hot.

Ingredients

2 medium-sized cauliflowers
1 tbsp carom seed
1 tbsp *garam masala*
1 tbsp red chilli powder
1 tbsp ginger-garlic paste
½ tsp turmeric powder
Salt to taste
8 tbsp oil
4 metal skewers.
Chaat masala for garnishing

Meat, Chicken and Seafood

Cerkez Tavugu (Chicken with Walnut Sauce)

Method

1. In a saucepan, combine the chicken, water and half teaspoon of the salt.
2. Bring to a boil over high heat. Reduce the heat to low, cover partially, and simmer for 30 minutes, or until the chicken is tender but not falling apart.
3. Remove the chicken pieces and boil the stock rapidly, uncovered, over high heat until reduced to 1½ cups.
4. Combine the walnuts, onions and stock. Blend in a blender at high speed for 15 seconds.
5. Add the bread, ½ teaspoon of the red chilli powder, the remaining salt, and a little bit of ground pepper. Blend at high speed until the mixture becomes a smooth puree.
6. When the chicken is cool enough to handle, remove the meat from the bones. Discard the bones and cut the chicken meat into strips.

Ingredients

1½ kg chicken, cut into 6 or 8 serving pieces
3 cups water
1½ tsp salt
1½ cup walnuts
½ cup finely chopped onions
3 slices of bread
1 tsp red chilli powder
Freshly ground black pepper

Garnish

¼ cup walnuts
½ tsp red chilli powder

Method

7. Place the chicken in a bowl and add 1½ cup of the walnut sauce, tossing the chicken about with a spoon to coat the pieces well.
8. Mound the chicken on a platter, pour the remaining sauce over it, and sprinkle with half teaspoon red chilli powder.
9. To make the garnish, pulverize the walnuts and red chilli in a mortar and pestle. Place a spoonful of the mixture at a time in a garlic press and squeeze the oil over the chicken.
10. Serve warm.

Chicken Marsala

Method

1. Beat the eggs with salt and pepper in a medium bowl.
2. Combine the breadcrumbs and Parmesan. Spread them on an aluminium foil.
3. Dip the chicken breasts in the beaten eggs and coat them with the breadcrumb mixture. Press the mixture onto the chicken with the palms of your hands. Let the coated chicken stand in a refrigerator for 10–15 minutes.
4. Melt the butter with oil in a large, heavy wok.
5. When the butter foams, add the chicken breasts. Cook over medium heat for 2–3 minutes on each side or until the chicken has a light golden crust.
6. Add the Marsala or port wine. Cover the wok* and reduce the heat. Simmer for 15–20 minutes, or until the chicken is tender. If the sauce looks too dry, add more wine. Turn the chicken several times during cooking.

Ingredients

4 boneless chicken breasts, halved

2 eggs

Salt and pepper to taste

1½ cups dry breadcrumbs ⅓ cup grated Parmesan cheese

¼ cup butter

2 tbsp olive oil

1 cup dry Marsala or port wine

Method

7. Place the chicken on a warm platter.
8. Taste and adjust the seasoning of the sauce, then spoon it over the chicken.
9. Serve immediately.

**or Kadhai*

Chicken Tahitian

Method

1. Preheat the oven to 325ºC.
2. Heat ¼ cup of the butter in a pan and cook the chicken until browned. Place in a shallow baking dish.
3. Heat the remaining butter with the pineapple-orange juice.
4. Add the ginger, salt and soy sauce.
5. Mix well and pour the sauce over the chicken.
6. Bake for 40 minutes (or longer if chicken pieces are larger), basting several times.
7. Serve hot with rice.

Ingredients

3 chicken breasts, split
½ cup butter
200 ml pineapple-orange juice
1 tsp ginger
½ tsp salt
1 tsp soy sauce
Rice, to serve

Chicken Teriyaki

Ingredients

1 kg chicken, cut into serving pieces

Marinade

½ cup soy sauce
¼ cup sugar
1 clove garlic, crushed
1 pinch MSG (optional)
¼ cup sake, sherry, or Mirin
¼ tsp grated fresh ginger

Method

1. Combine the marinade ingredients and pour over the chicken pieces. Marinate for 2 hours or longer, turning the pieces occasionally.
2. Preheat the oven to 180ºC.
3. Place the chicken pieces on a greased cookie sheet and bake for about 35 minutes.
4. Turn the pieces over, brush with the drippings, and bake for another 40 minutes, for a total cooking time of 1 hour and 15 minutes.
5. To glaze, brush with drippings. Serve hot.

Grilled Fish with Béarnaise Sauce

Method

1. Wash and dry the fillets, season with salt and pepper and moisten with 1 teaspoon of olive oil.
2. Sprinkle one side of the fillets with breadcrumbs, pressing down to make the breadcrumbs adhere.
3. Put under a hot broiler, breaded side up. Baste with butter occasionally.
4. When one side is done, turn carefully and cook the other side.
5. Arrange the cooked fillets on a long hot dish, the non-breaded side up.
6. Sprinkle with lemon juice, surround with the small grilled tomatoes. Season with salt and pepper.
7. Heap half a tablespoon of rice on each tomato.
8. For the sauce, in a double boiler top, combine the first 4 ingredients of the Béarnaise sauce. Over a high heat, heat to boiling.

Ingredients

- 1 kg fish fillet
- 1 cup fresh breadcrumbs
- 1 10 gms butter
- Salt and pepper to taste
- 1 lemon
- 6 small tomatoes, grilled
- 3 tbsp cooked rice
- Olive oil

Béarnaise Sauce

- 2 tbsp red wine vinegar
- 1½ tsp chopped spring onion
- 1½ tsp tarragon
- ⅛ tsp cracked black pepper
- 4 egg yolks
- ¾ cup butter, softened
- 1 tbsp chopped parsley

Method

9. Boil until the vinegar is reduced to about 1 tablespoon.
10. Place the double boiler top over the double boiler bottom containing hot, not boiling, water. As an option, you could heat a pan, remove from heat and then go on to step 11.
11. Add the egg yolks and cook, whisking constantly until slightly thickened.
12. Add the butter, about 2 tablespoons at a time, beating constantly with a whisk, until the butter is melted and the mixture is thickened.
13. Stir in the parsley.
14. Pour about 1 tablespoon of sauce over each fillet. Serve the rest of the sauce separately.

Guisado Espanol (Stew)

Method

1. In a small fry pan heat the olive oil and cook the onions, garlic and parsley until brown, for about 10 minutes. Set aside.
2. In a hot, heavy pot add the meat and cook till it is brown on all sides.
3. Add the onion mixture (as in step 1), salt, pepper, capsicums, carrots, the stock, and the wine.
4. Bring to a boil. Cover the pot tightly and turn the heat down to a bare simmer. Cook for 45 minutes or until the meat is almost tender.
5. Add the potatoes and mushrooms.
6. Turn the heat up to moderate and cook until the potatoes are done, for about ½ hour more.
7. Correct the seasoning with salt and pepper If necessary.
8. Sprinkle with pimiento strips and serve.

Note : pressure cooking may be expeditious but will lose some of the taste.

Ingredients

¼ cup olive oil
3 onions, chopped
2 cloves garlic, minced
2 tbsp minced parsley
900 gms mutton, cut into 1" cubes
Salt and pepper to taste
3 capsicums, cut in strips
½ cup sliced carrots
2½ cups chicken stock
1½ cup red wine
½ cup button mushrooms, halved
4 potatoes, peeled and quartered
3 tbsp pimiento, cut in strips

Lamb Rendang

Ingredients

750	gms boneless lamb, cut into bite-size pieces Peel of ½ lemon, minced
1	onion, minced
½	tsp turmeric powder
2	tbsp chilli powder
2	tsp salt
1	cup desiccated coconut
2	cups coconut milk
1	tsp sugar
8	tbsp oil

Method

1. Spread the coconut over the surface of a large heavy pan and place over high heat. Stir continuously and when the coconut becomes golden brown, remove from the heat and pound into a fine powder.
2. Heat the oil in a large heavy pan. When the oil is hot, toss in the minced onion and lemon peel. Stir well and add the chilli powder, turmeric and salt.
3. Stir-fry for 1 minute, then add the lamb and continue to fry until the meat is well coated with the spices and is browned.
4. Pour in the coconut milk, sugar and powdered coconut.
5. Continue to simmer gently, uncovered, until the lamb is cooked, and the liquid has evaporated.
6. Serve immediately.

Ayam Panggang (Grilled Chicken-breasts)

Ingredients

4	chicken breasts, cut into 4 pieces
2	onions, chopped
1″	ginger, chopped
3	cloves garlic, chopped
2	green chillies, chopped
2	cups coconut milk
1	tsp turmeric paste
2	tsp salt

Method

1. Place the onions, ginger, garlic, and green chillies in an electric blender.
2. Add the turmeric paste and ½ cup of the coconut milk.
3. Blend thoroughly to make a thick paste.
4. Add the rest of the coconut milk and the salt.
5. Pour the blended ingredients into a heavy pan and bring to a boil.
6. Add the chicken pieces and simmer until all the liquid has evaporated.
7. Remove the chicken pieces, place under a hot grill and cook for 5–6 minutes on each side until they are golden brown.
8. Serve hot.

Roast Leg of Lamb

Ingredients

- 3-3½ kg leg of lamb
- 2 cloves garlic, cut into slivers
- 2 tbsp chopped fresh ginger
- 6 cloves garlic
- Seeds of 3 cardamom pods
- ¼ tsp cinnamon
- 8 cloves
- 1 tsp cumin seeds
- 1 tsp turmeric powder
- ¼ tsp red chilli powder
- 4 tsp salt
- ¼ cup fresh lemon juice
- ¼ cup yoghurt
- ¼ tsp freshly ground black Pepper
- ½ tsp saffron threads
- 3 tbsp boiling water

Method

1. With a sharp knife, cut ½-inch long and 1-inch deep incisions in the lamb leg and insert a sliver of garlic in each.
2. Combine the next 10 ingredients (ginger through lemon juice) and blend until the mixture becomes a smooth puree.
3. Rub the spice puree over the entire outer surface of the lamb leg, pressing it as deeply into the incisions as possible.
4. Let it stand at room temperature for 30 minutes.
5. Mix the yoghurt and black pepper and spread evenly over the lamb.
6. Cover and marinate in a cool place for about 24 hours, or in the refrigerator for 48 hours.
7. Preheat the oven to 200°C.
8. Soak the saffron threads in the boiling water for 15 minutes and pour the mixture over the lamb.

Method

9. Roast the lamb uncovered for 25 minutes. Then reduce the heat to over 190°C and roast for another 2 hours or until done. Turn the lamb over once or twice, basting occasionally.
10. Remove to a heated platter and let stand for 20 minutes before carving.

Shepherd's Pie

Ingredients

- 450 gms minced lamb
- 1 small onion, chopped
- ¼ cup flour
- ½ cup meat stock
- A pinch of marjoram
- 1 tsp chopped parsley
- Salt and pepper to taste
- 1 tsp Worcestershire sauce
- 1 tbsp oil
- 450 gms boiled and mashed potatoes

Method

1. Heat the oil in a pan and fry the onion and the meat till brown.
2. Stir in the flour and the stock.
3. Add the parsley, marjoram, salt, and pepper to taste.
4. Blend in the Worcestershire sauce.
5. Put the meat mixture into a greased baking dish.
6. Place a layer of mashed potatoes over the meat mixture. Decorate by riffling the surface with a fork.
7. Preheat the oven to 180°C.
8. Bake for about 45 minutes or until the top is golden brown. Let it rest for 5–10 minutes before serving.

Grilled Sesame Chicken

Method

1. Toast the sesame seeds till they turn just brown and grind them.
2. Prepare a marinade by mixing the sherry, oil, soy sauce, vinegar, sugar, and the ground sesame seeds.
3. Marinate the chicken in this for at least 30 minutes.
4. Transfer the chicken onto a baking tray and place in a preheated grill on high heat. Turn over the chicken pieces after every six minutes, basting frequently with the marinade and sesame oil, till the chicken is cooked thoroughly.
5. Remove and slice each breast diagonally into 6–8 strips and serve on individual plates garnished with a lemon wedge and spring onions.

Ingredients

6	boneless chicken breasts
2	tbsp sesame seeds
¾	cup dry sherry
2	tbsp salad oil
2	tbsp sesame oil
3	tbsp soy sauce
1½	tbsp vinegar
1	tbsp sugar
1	lemon, cut into wedges
6	spring onions, trimmed and cut

Escabeche (Pickled Fish)

Ingredients

- 3 tbsp flour
- 1 tsp salt
- 900 gms fish fillets
- ⅔ cup olive oil
- 2 large onions, sliced
- 1 red capsicum, cored, seeded and sliced
- 2 garlic cloves, chopped
- 1 red chilli pepper, seeded and chopped
- 3 bay leaves
- ¼ tsp peppercorns
- 1¼ cup red wine vinegar

Method

1. Mix together flour and 1 teaspoon salt and use this to coat the fish fillets.
2. Heat 6 tablespoons of the oil in a heavy pan.
3. Add the fish and fry for 4–5 minutes on each side or until browned and cooked through. Drain the fish on paper towels.
4. Heat the remaining oil, add the onions and fry until softened.
5. Stir in the red capsicum, garlic, chilli pepper, bay leaves, peppercorns, and vinegar.
6. Bring to a boil and simmer for 2 minutes.
7. Arrange the fish in a serving dish. Pour over the vinegar mixture and cover.
8. Cool, then place in the refrigerator. Leave to marinate for 2–3 days.
9. Serve as appetizer or main course.

Wrapped Steamed Fish

Method

1. Grind together the garlic, green chillies, lemon peel, turmeric, salt, pepper, desiccated coconut, and a little of the coconut milk. Blend until you have a smooth paste.
2. Cut 4 pieces of aluminium foil large enough to wrap up each fillet.
3. Heat the remaining coconut milk in a saucepan. Do not let it boil.
4. Remove from the heat and add the blended paste. Stir well.
5. Lay out each sheet of foil on your worktop. Spread some of the coconut paste on each.
6. Place the strips of fillet on top and spread the remaining paste evenly over the four fillets. Fold up the foil and seal to make 4 parcels.
7. Place the parcels in a steamer and steam for 30 minutes.
8. Serve straight from the wrappers.

Ingredients

4 large white fish fillets, cut into thin strips
2 cloves garlic
3 fresh green chillies
Peel of ½ lemon
1 tsp turmeric powder
2 tsp salt
½ tsp freshly ground pepper
4 tbsp desiccated coconut
1 cup coconut milk

Sweet and Sour Ham Balls

Ingredients

- 450 gms ham, minced
- 450 gms chicken mince
- 1 can water chestnuts, drained and finely chopped (optional)
- ¼ cup milk
- 1 egg, slightly beaten
- 1 cup brown sugar
- ½ cup white vinegar
- ½ cup water
- ½ tsp dry mustard

Method

1. Preheat the oven to 180°C.
2. Mix the first 5 ingredients and roll them into small balls.
3. Place them in a shallow pan large enough to hold all the meatballs in one layer.
4. Mix together the remaining ingredients and bring to a boil. Pour over the meatballs.
5. Bake for 1 hour, basting several times.
6. Serve hot.

Chicken Vindaloo

Method

1. Combine all the ingredients of the marinade and mix in the chicken. Marinate the chicken for at least 1 hour.
2. Prepare the paste by grinding together the coriander and cumin powder, cinnamon, cloves, peppercorns, red chillies, garlic, and ginger. Add the vinegar 1 tablespoon at a time and blend to a fine paste.
3. Heat the oil in a pan. Fry the onions till translucent.
4. Add the turmeric and chilli powder and stir-fry briefly.
5. Add the paste. Fry for a few minutes.
6. Add the chicken along with all the marinade juices. Stir well so that the chicken pieces are well coated with the spices.
7. Add sufficient water and salt to taste, and bring to boil.
8. Simmer till the chicken is well done.
9. Serve hot with steamed basmati rice or Indian flatbreads.

Ingredients

1 kg chicken

Marinade

3 tbsp vinegar
¼ tsp Kashmiri red chilli powder
½ tsp pepper
Salt to taste
1 tsp tamarind extract

Paste

2 tbsp coriander powder
1 tbsp cumin powder
1" piece cinnamon
6 cloves
1 Star Anise
1 tsp peppercorn
6 whole red chillies
10 cloves garlic, chopped
1" ginger, chopped
3 tbsp vinegar
Oil
3 medium onions, finely chopped
½ tsp turmeric powder
½ tsp Kashmiri red chilli powder
Salt to taste

Island Fish Curry

Ingredients

4	fish fillets
½"	ginger, chopped
1	tsp chopped garlic
2	tomatoes, chopped
½	tsp turmeric powder
½	tsp cumin seed
½	tsp coriander powder
	Red chilli powder to taste
	Salt to taste
1	cup coconut milk
1	lemon
2	tbsp oil
	Boiled rice, to serve

Method

1. Heat the oil in a pan. On low heat, add the ginger and garlic. Cook till light brown.
2. Add the tomatoes and mash them. Stir well and cook for 5–6 minutes.
3. Add all the spices and cook for some time.
4. Add half the coconut milk and the fish pieces.
5. After 3 minutes add the remaining coconut milk
6. Cook for another 5 minutes. Add the lemon juice.
7. Serve hot with boiled rice.

Prawns Louisiana Style

Method

1. Heat the butter. Add the onions and cook for 5 minutes, stirring constantly. Do not brown the onions.
2. Add the prawns, rice and cream.
3. When thoroughly heated, add the salt, celery salt and red chilli powder to taste.
4. Serve hot.

Ingredients

½ cup butter
½ cup chopped onion
5 cups cooked prawns
5 cups hot boiled rice
5 cups cream
3 tsp salt
2 tsp celery salt
Red chilli powder

Stuffed Capsicum

Ingredients

4 capsicum
680 gms minced mutton
1 egg, beaten
½ onion, chopped fine
2 cups cooked rice
170 gms shredded Cheddar cheese
2 tsp Worcestershire sauce
1 tsp tarragon
A dash of black pepper
Salt to taste

Method

1. Preheat the oven to 180°C.
2. Mix the meat, egg and onion in a large bowl.
3. Fold in the rice, cheese, Worcestershire sauce, and spices.
4. Wash the capsicum, removing the seeds and tops. Drain well.
5. Stuff the capsicum with the meat mixture.
6. Bake, uncovered, in a shallow dish for 50 minutes.
7. Serve when ready.

Swedish Meatballs

Method

1. Heat 1 teaspoon butter in a pan. Cook the onions.
2. Soak the breadcrumbs in milk.
3. Mix the mince, breadcrumbs, salt, pepper, allspice, and fried onion.
4. Form into meatballs.
5. Heat the remaining butter and oil together. Add the meatballs and cook over gentle heat, turning frequently, about 10 minutes. Remove the meatballs to a small casserole and keep hot.
6. Add the flour to the drippings in the pan and stir for 1 minute.
7. Stir in the stock and scrape up the browned bits in the pan.
8. Add the cream, coriander leaves and mustard and cook for 2–3 minutes.
9. Adjust the seasonings and pour the sauce over the meatballs.
10. Serve with rice, noodles, or mashed potatoes.

Ingredients

½ cup finely chopped onion
2 tbsp plus 1 tsp butter
½ cup fresh breadcrumbs
½ cup milk
450 gms minced meat
Salt and pepper
⅛ tsp allspice
1 tbsp oil
1½ tbsp flour
1 cup chicken stock
1 cup heavy cream
2 tbsp chopped fresh coriander leaves
1 tsp mustard paste
Rice, noodles, or mashed pota toes to serve

Bread and Rice

Paneer (Cottage Cheese) Naan

Method

1. Mix the sugar and yeast in 1 cup of warm water. Stir until the yeast dissolves. Cover and wait for about 5–7 minutes until the mixture is full of froth.
2. Add this liquid along with the yoghurt, clarified butter and salt to the flour.
3. Make a soft dough by adding some more warm water. Knead the dough for at least 6–7 minutes.
4. Keep the dough under a wet cloth for 30 minutes. Knead again for 1 minute.
5. Mix the ingredients for the stuffing well.
6. Divide the dough into 20 small balls.
7. Flatten the balls and then put 1 teaspoon of the filling in the centre of each round. Close the edges and roll into an oblong shape.
8. Grease a pressure cooker very lightly with oil. Place the cooker on the gas flame upside down.

Ingredients

Dough

- 500 gms flour, sieved
- 1½ tsp sugar
- 20 gms fresh yeast or 2 tsp dry yeast
- 2 tbsp curd
- 25 gms clarified butter
- 1 tsp salt

Stuffing

- 100 gms grated cottage cheese
- 1 onion, chopped
- 3–4 green chillies, chopped
- 2 tbsp chopped fresh coriander leaves
- Salt to taste

Serving

- 50 gms butter

Method

9. Take each naan, apply a little water on one side and stick the wet side around the inside of the pressure cooker.
10. Cook till brown spots appear. Remove and apply butter.
11. Repeat for the rest of the dough. You can cook 3–4 naans at one time.
12. Apply butter and serve hot.

Mexican Rice

Method

1. Wash the rice thoroughly and drain well.
2. Heat the oil for about one minute. Add the rice and fry till brown.
3. Drain the excess oil, leaving enough to fry the rest of the ingredients.
4. Add the onions and garlic; mix well.
5. Add the tomato sauce or the fresh tomato and mix for about half a minute.
6. Add a dash of tabasco and worcestershire sauce.
7. Add the water and salt to taste, bring to a boil. Cover pan and lower the flame.
8. Cook for 20–30 minutes.
9. Serve hot.

Ingredients

- 2 cups rice
- 2 tbsp oil
- ¼ diced onion
- 1 clove garlic, minced
- 2 tbsp tomato sauce or 1 tomato, finely chopped
- 4 cups water
- Salt to taste

Creole Red Beans with Rice

Ingredients

- 750 gms *rajma* (red kidney beans)
- 750 gms mutton, cut in small pieces
- 1 tbsp olive oil
- 1 large onion, finely chopped
- 3 cloves garlic, finely chopped
- 1½ tsp thyme
- 1½ tsp oregano
- 1 bay leaf
- 3 tbsp tomato paste
- Salt and freshly ground pepper to taste
- 1 tsp Tabasco sauce, or to taste
- 450 gms sausage, chopped into 1" pieces
- 2 cups rice, cooked
- 1 onion, chopped
- Olive oil and red pepper vinegar (optional)

Method

1. Heat the olive oil. Sauté the onions until they are soft but not brown.
2. Add *rajma* and all the remaining ingredients except the sausage, rice and onion.
3. Add enough water to just cover the beans. Bring to a boil, cover tightly and lower the heat to simmer. Stir every 10 minutes or so and add more water as needed. Usually, *rajma* should take about 1½ to 2 hours to become soft yet remain whole. The sauce should be quite thick.
4. About 30 minutes before the beans have fully cooked, add the sausage.
5. Serve the beans on a bed of rice, with the chopped onion sprinkled on top.
6. Olive oil and Red pepper vinegar can be added to taste at the table.

Tip: Soak *Rajma* in water the night before to get good results.

Tip: Pressure cooking will cut down time but may compromise on taste.

Gosht Biryani

Method

1. Mix together the yoghurt, chilli powder, coriander powder, ginger-garlic paste, and salt.
2. Marinate the meat in the yoghurt mixture for 30 minutes.
3. Heat the clarified butter. Add whole *garam masala* and fry till it crackles.
4. Add the onions. Cook till brown.
5. Add the marinated mutton and cook over low heat till meat is tender. Add water as and when required.
6. To cook the rice, boil the milk and water together.
7. Add the rice, whole *garam masala* and salt.
8. Cook till the rice is almost done.
9. In a handi, a round deep cooking vessel, place alternate layers of rice and mutton, starting and ending with rice.

Ingredients

600 gms mutton, cut into cubes
300 gms yoghurt
1 tsp red chilli powder
1 tsp coriander powder
2 tsp ginger-garlic paste
1 tsp salt, or to taste
100 gms clarified butter
1 tsp whole *garam masala*
150 gms onions, sliced rice
500 gms Basmati rice
500 ml milk
500 ml water
1 tsp whole *garam masala*
Salt to taste

Garnish

a pinch of saffron
1 tbsp milk
1 tsp mint
1 tsp julienned ginger
2 tsp chopped fresh coriander leaves
20 gms split cashew nut

Method

10. Garnish with mint, ginger juliennes, coriander leaves, and cashew nut between each layer.
11. Place the cover of the handi. Seal the sides of the cover with flour dough.
12. Place burning charcoal on the cover of the handi or place the handi in a hot oven. Cook for 15–20 minutes.
13. Open the handi right on the table and serve hot.
14. Top it with a pinch of saffron mixed with a tablespoon of milk

Pasta with Gorgonzola*

Method

1. Bring a large pan of salted water to boil for the pasta.
2. Cook the pasta and drain well.
3. Combine the cream, butter, pepper, and Gorgonzola in a saucepan. Melt them together over low heat. Do not boil.
4. Toss the pasta with the cheese sauce and half of the Parmesan.
5. Serve hot garnished with the remaining cheese.

*or any other blue cheese

Ingredients

450 gms pasta
1 cup whipping cream
¼ cup butter
¼ tsp cayenne pepper
110 gms Gorgonzola cheese
110 gms Parmesan cheese, grated

Walnut flavoured Pasta

Ingredients

- 2 cups walnuts
- 2 cloves garlic
- 4 tbsp lemon juice
- ½ cup fresh parsley
- 340 gms ricotta cheese
- 1 cup milk
- 1 tsp salt
- ¼ tsp black pepper
- 2 tsp oregano
- 340 gms pasta, freshly cooked and drained

Method

1. Process the walnuts, garlic and lemon juice in a blender till the ingredients are chopped fine.
2. Add the rest of the ingredients (except pasta) to the blender and process until flecked with green.
3. Add the mixture to the hot pasta in a large bowl and toss.
4. Serve immediately.

5-minute Noodles

Method

1. Heat 3 tablespoons of the oil in a frying pan.
2. Add the garlic and cook over medium heat until the garlic is golden brown.
3. Add the noodles and stir for 2 minutes.
4. Make a well in the middle of the noodles, pour in the remaining oil, add the beaten egg and stir until the egg is almost cooked.
5. Add the soy sauce and sugar. Mix everything together.
6. Season to taste.
7. Add the bean sprouts (optional, otherwise use fresh coriander) and stir for one minute more.
8. Serve hot.

Ingredients

- 4 tbsp oil
- 2 cloves garlic, finely chopped
- 2 cups cooked noodles
- 1 egg, beaten
- 3 tbsp soy sauce
- 1 tsp sugar
- 1 cup bean sprouts
- Salt and black pepper to taste

Phad Thai

Ingredients

- 60 ml oil
- 50 gms tofu or cottage cheese, thinly sliced into strips
- 1 red chilli, deseeded and finely sliced
- 1 clove garlic, crushed
- 150 gms cellophane noodles
- 1 egg
- 1 tbsp soy sauce
- A pinch of sugar
- 2 tbsp chopped peanuts
- 200 gms bean sprouts
- 1 tbsp chopped fresh coriander leaves
- 1 lime, cut into wedges

Method

1. Cover the noodles with boiling water and allow to soak for 5 minutes only, until pliable. Drain and set aside.
2. Heat 2 tablespoons of oil in a wok. Add the tofu and fry over a medium heat until heated through. Set aside, and keep warm.
3. Add the remaining oil to the pan. Add the garlic and chilli and fry until brown.
4. Add the drained noodles and cook until heated through.
5. Push the noodles to the sides of the pan and break the egg into the centre. Cook, mixing gently until it begins to set, then break it up and mix it into the noodles.
6. Add the soy sauce and sugar; mix well.
7. Stir in the tofu, bean sprouts, peanuts, and coriander, mixing well.
8. Cook for 3–4 minutes until the bean sprouts are heated through.
9. Transfer to a serving platter and garnish with lime wedges.

Desserts

Desserts

Chocolate Madeleines

Method

1. Preheat the oven to 180ºC.
2. Melt the butter and the semi-sweet chocolate in a double boiler; let cool.
3. Sift the flour with cocoa and salt.
4. Break the eggs into a bowl and place the bowl over hot water. Whisk in the sugar. Continue whisking until the eggs are warm.
5. Remove the bowl from the water and beat the eggs and sugar for 6–8 minutes, until very thick and light in colour.
6. Lightly fold in the chocolate mixture and the flour mixture, alternately in thirds. Should be very well combined.
7. Bake in oiled madeleine tins for 13–15 minutes, until done (test as you would for a cake).
8. When cooled, dust the madeleines with a mixture of cocoa and confectioners' sugar. Transfer to a rack to cool. Serve slightly warm or at room temperature.

Ingredients

¾ cup butter
100 gms semi-sweet chocolate
1 cup flour
2 tbsp cocoa
A pinch of salt
4 eggs
⅔ cup sugar
Madeleine tins.

Dusting

1 tsp cocoa
2 tbsp confectioners' sugar

Coffee-Coffee Cake

Ingredients

- 1 cup raisins
- ⅔ cup strong coffee, cooled
- ⅔ cup unsalted butter
- 1 cup sugar
- 2 eggs
- 1½ cups flour
- ½ tsp baking powder
- ½ tsp baking soda
- ½ tsp cinnamon
- ¼ tsp nutmeg

Icing

- 1 cup confectioners' sugar
- 7–9 tsp strong coffee, cooled

Method

1. Soak the raisins in coffee for an hour or two.
2. Preheat the oven to 180°C.
3. Grease a baking tin.
4. Cream the butter and sugar together.
5. Add the eggs one at a time.
6. Sift together the dry ingredients.
7. Alternately add the dry ingredients and the coffee-raisin mixture to the batter.
8. Spread the batter in a baking tin and bake for about 25 minutes.
9. To make the icing, mix the coffee with the sugar.
10. Spread the icing over the cake and cut immediately, as icing hardens fast. While slicing the cake, keep dipping the knife in coffee.

Crepes Suzette

Method

1. Mix the eggs with flour, sugar and salt.
2. Add the milk until the batter reaches the consistency of condensed milk. Beat until smooth.
3. Heat an oiled griddle.
4. Pour about 2 tablespoons of the batter onto the griddle, tilting quickly to distribute the batter evenly.
5. Cook the crepe 1 minute or so, until brown, then turn and brown the other side. Remove.
6. Oil the griddle and repeat with the rest of the batter. Keep the cooked crepes warm in a towel.
7. To make the sauce, melt the butter. Add the sugar and mix well.
8. Add the juice of lemon and orange and the peels. Simmer until the peels are transparent.

Ingredients

2 eggs
¾ cup flour, sifted
A pinch of salt
1 tsp sugar
Milk

Sauce

½ cup butter
½ cup sugar
Juice of ½ lemon
Juice of 1 orange
Peel of 3 oranges, thinly slivered
Peel of 1 lemon, thinly slivered
25 ml Cointreau
25 ml Grand Marnier (or dark rum)
60 ml brandy

Method

9. Place the crepes one at a time in this sauce and fold into halves and then quarters. Slide each crepe to the very edge of the pan. Tilt the pan slightly so the sauce runs back into the centre, then add the next crepe.
10. Repeat until all the crepes are dipped in the sauce.
11. Pour the Cointreau, Grand Marnier and then the brandy evenly over the crepes.
12. Tip the pan slightly so that the flame will ignite the brandy.
13. Level the pan and move in a light forward and backward motion until the flame on the crepes dies down.
14. Serve the crepes on warm plates, spooning some of the remaining sauce over them.

Dobosh Torte

Method

1. Preheat the oven to 180ºC.
2. Grease three 8-inch circular cake tins.
3. Beat the egg yolks and sugar until well blended. Refrigerate.
4. Sift separately the flour and the baking powder.
5. Beat the egg whites until stiff peaks form.
6. Fold alternately the flour mixture and the egg whites into the egg yolk-sugar mixture, using about a third each time.
7. Pour the batter into the prepared tins.
8. Bake until the cakes are light golden brown.
9. Let the cakes stand and cool completely.
10. Once cool, each cake can be sliced in half, horizontally, so that there are 6 layers of the cake.
11. For frosting, beat the ingredients together until smooth.

Ingredients

- 12 eggs, separated
- 1 cup sugar
- 12 tbsp flour
- 2 tsp baking powder

Frosting

- 1½ cup unsalted butter
- 450 gms powdered sugar
- 3 squares bitter chocolate, melted
- 3 egg yolks
- 3 tbsp cold, black coffee

Method

12. Spread frosting on each layer of the cake and stack one on top of the other. Continue frosting the top and the sides of the cake until completely covered. Leave the cake to season for 6 hours in the refrigerator before serving.

Basboussa

Method

1. Preheat the oven to 180ºC.
2. Mix the sugar, coconut and semolina.
3. Combine the milk and butter and bring to a boil.
4. Add the semolina mixture to the boiling milk. Remove from heat.
5. Add the yoghurt and mix well.
6. Pour into a greased baking tray.
7. Bake for about 35 minutes, until golden-yellow.
8. Remove from the oven and sprinkle with slivered almonds. Press the nuts gently into the baked surface.
9. Leave the basboussa to cool for 1 hour.
10. To make the syrup, combine the sugar, water and lemon juice. Bring to a boil.
11. Add the clarified butter.
12. Simmer for about 15 minutes and cool.
13. Once the basboussa is cool soak with the cold sugar syrup.
14. Cut into pieces and serve warm or cold.

Ingredients

2 cups semolina
1 cup sugar
1 cup coconut flakes
1 cup clarified butter
1 cup milk
½ tbsp yoghurt
½ cup slivered almonds

Syrup

1 cup sugar
1 cup water
2 tbsp lemon juice
1 tbsp clarified butter

Rasgulla

Ingredients

1	litre milk
½	tsp citric acid
1½	cup sugar
4	cups water

Method

1. Bring the milk to a boil.
2. Add the citric acid* dissolved in some water and stir the milk slowly. The milk will curdle to produce cottage cheese. Keep the mixture in this state for 5 minutes.
3. Heat the sugar and water in a wide saucepan and bring to a boil.
4. Strain the curdled milk through a muslin cloth.
5. Wash the cottage cheese in the cloth under cold running water. Drain out excess water.
6. Knead the cottage cheese well and make 10–12 equal sized balls from it.
7. Put them into the sugar syrup. Cover with a perforated lid.
8. Boil for about 13–15 minutes. Remove the pan from the heat.
9. Chill for at least 4–5 hours before serving.

*(you can use lime juice too)

Banket (Almond Pastry)

Ingredients

Dough

450 gms butter
4 cups flour
1 cup cold water
½ tsp cream of tartar

Filling

450 gms almond paste
2 cups sugar
3 eggs
1 tsp almond essence
2 egg whites, slightly beaten

Method

1. Mix all the ingredients of the dough thoroughly and quickly.
2. Separate into four parts. Chill overnight.
3. Mix the filling ingredients. Chill.
4. Preheat the oven to 225°C.
5. Take each part of the dough, roll into an elongated strip and cut in half the long way.
6. Each part of the dough makes two strips of banket.
7. Put an eighth of the filling in long cylindrical shape down the centre of each strip. Fold the ends over first. Using water to seal the edges, fold one long side of the dough over the filling and then the other.
8. Place on a cookie sheet seam side down (four per cookie sheet).
9. Pierce the top of the rolls 4 or 5 times with a fork and brush with egg white.
10. Bake for 25–30 minutes, until golden brown. Cool the sheets on wire racks. When the bankets are cool, gently release from the sheets to serve.

Meringues

Ingredients

2 egg whites
50 gms sugar
50 gms castor sugar
150 ml whipped cream

Method

1. Preheat the oven to 150ºC.
2. Line the baking sheet with non-stick paper.
3. Whisk the egg whites till very stiff.
4. Fold in the sugar and whisk again till stiff.
5. Fold in the castor sugar very lightly, using a metal spoon.
6. Put spoonfuls of the mixture onto the baking sheet and bake for 30 minutes. When the meringues begin to brown, open the oven door a little.
7. Cool on wire rack and sandwich with whipped cream.

Gulab Jamun

Method

1. Combine the khoya, cottage cheese, flour, semolina, baking powder, cardamom powder, nutmeg powder, and a little bit of the water.
2. Mix well.
3. Heat the clarified butter in a wok.
4. In another wok, heat the sugar syrup.
5. Shape the khoya mixture into long cigar like shapes.
6. Fry the khoya balls on a slow fire. Keep stirring gently. Once the balls float on top, increase the heat.
7. Remove when brown in colour.
8. Put the fried jamuns in the hot syrup.
9. Serve hot or cold garnished with chopped nuts.

Ingredients

500 gms khoya, grated
100 gms cottage cheese
25 gms flour
25 gms semolina
A pinch of baking powder
A pinch of cardamom powder
A pinch of nutmeg powder
Clarified butter for frying
1 litre sugar syrup
Chopped almonds, pistachio nuts for garnishing

Kugel (Noodle Pudding)

Ingredients

- 3 eggs
- 340 gms cottage cheese
- 2 cups milk
- Raisins to taste
- 1 tsp vanilla essence
- ¼ –½ cup sugar
- 225 gms broad noodles
- 110 gms butter, melted
- Crushed cornflakes
- Cinnamon powder
- Powdered sugar

Method

1. Preheat the oven to 180°C.
2. Beat the eggs in a large bowl.
3. Add the cottage cheese, milk, raisins, sugar, and vanilla essence.
4. Mix well and add the noodles.
5. Add the butter.
6. Pour into a baking dish. Top with the crushed cornflakes and sprinkle cinnamon and sugar evenly over the top.
7. Bake for 1 hour.

Can be served hot or cold.

Rizogalo (Rice Pudding)

Ingredients

6 cups milk
⅔ cup rice
1 cup sugar
2 eggs, beaten
400 gms milk powder
Cinnamon powder

Method

1. In a large saucepan, blend the milk, rice and sugar. Do not stir.
2. Cover and cook over medium low flame until the mixture begins to steam (about 20 minutes). Do not let it boil over.
3. Uncover, stir and lower flame to simmer.
4. Cover loosely and cook for 45 minutes, until the rice is tender, stirring frequently.
5. Mix the beaten eggs with milk powder and gradually add to the rice mixture.
6. Stir constantly until the mixture thickens (about 20 minutes). Do not let the mixture boil.
7. Ladle into a large bowl. Sprinkle with the cinnamon powder.
8. Let cool and refrigerate for a few hours or overnight before serving.

Coconut Custard

Ingredients

4 eggs
1½ cup sugar
A pinch of salt
2 cups coconut milk
1 tbsp desiccated coconut

Method

1. Preheat the oven to 180°C.
2. Beat the eggs, sugar and salt until light and frothy.
3. Add the coconut milk and pour into a large bowl.
4. Cover the bowl with aluminium foil, place in a shallow pan of hot water, and bake for 25 minutes or until the custard is set.
5. Cool and sprinkle with desiccated coconut before serving.

Silk and Satin Chocolate Mousse

Method

1. Melt the chocolates together and cool.
2. Beat the egg whites until foamy and double in volume.
3. Add the sugar slowly, beating until stiff peaks form.
4. Beat ½ cup of the whipping cream until stiff.
5. Separately, beat the egg yolks until thick and light.
6. Add the cooled chocolate slowly to the egg yolks. Blend well.
7. Beat in the brandy.
8. Beat in about ¼ of the egg whites.
9. Stir in the remaining whites lightly until no streaks of white remain.
10. Fold in the whipped cream.
11. Chill until firm, at least for 1 hour.
12. Whip the remaining cream. Garnish the mousse with it before serving.

Ingredients

- 60 gms unsweetened chocolate
- 120 gms semi-sweet chocolate
- 6 eggs, separated
- ¼ cup sugar
- 1 cup whipping cream
- 2 Tbsp brandy

Halwa

Ingredients

1 cup semolina flour
4 tbsp clarified butter
6–7 tbsp sugar
4 cups milk
Chopped almonds, pistachio nuts and raisins for garnishing

Method

1. Melt the clarified butter in a pan on a mild flame for a few minutes.
2. Add the flour to this. Stir till the flour is brown in colour.
3. Add the milk and sugar to this mixture.
4. Stir this mixture on a mild flame for 15 minutes till it becomes thick.
5. Garnish with raisins, almonds and pistachio.
6. Serve hot.

Flan

Method

1. Melt the sugar in the metal ring mould by slowly heating until the sugar liquefies.
2. Coat the ring by rotating it over the stove. Set the mould aside.
3. In a large bowl combine the condensed milk, eggs and vanilla.
4. Pour the mixture into the ring mould. Cover tightly with an aluminium foil.
5. Place the ring mould in a large pan filled with water. Boil slowly for 1½ hours, replenishing the water as needed.
6. Remove and invert the mould immediately onto a serving plate.
7. Serve cold, garnished with whipped cream.

Ingredients

2 tbsp sugar
2 cans condensed milk
4 eggs beaten
2 tbsp vanilla essence
A metal ring mould
Whipped cream for garnishing

Mysore Pak

Ingredients

1	cup gram flour
2½	cups sugar
2½	cups clarified butter

Method

1. Heat 1 cup of the clarified butter in a pan.
2. Add the gram flour and keep stirring it till it is a little brown. Keep aside.
3. Heat the sugar on a medium heat adding enough quantity of water to cover the sugar. After it has boiled for a while, carefully take a bit of the syrup on the tip of your forefinger and press it against your thumb. Gently pull the two fingers apart a little (about half an inch) to see whether the syrup is forming a single thread between the two fingers. This is a syrup of one thread consistency.
4. When the syrup reaches the desired consistency, strain it to remove the scum. Keep aside.
5. Heat the remaining 1½ cup of the clarified butter. On a low heat, add the roasted besan and the sugar syrup.
6. Keep stirring till the clarified butter separates and floats on top.

Method

7. Pour the mixture onto a greased plate and spread it evenly.
8. Cut into pieces.
9. The Mysore Pak can be stored in an airtight container.

Moong Dal Halwa

Ingredients

1 cup polished green gram
¾ cup clarified butter
¾ cup sugar
2 cups milk
2 tbsp grated almonds
2 tbsp raisin
2 tbsp cashew nuts, roasted
¼ cup khoya, grated

Method

1. Soak the green gram (*moong dal*) overnight.
2. Strain it in the morning and grind it in a mixie. Make sure that the mixture is a little grainy.
3. Take ¾ tablespoon of the clarified butter and heat it.
4. Add the ground paste and stir continuously so that it does not stick.
5. Keep adding a spoon of clarified butter and continue stirring.
6. Cook till golden in colour.
7. Make a syrup by boiling the sugar and milk in low flame for about 30 minutes..
8. Add the syrup to the roasted gram.
9. Cook for 5–6 minutes.
10. Garnish with dry fruits and *khoya*.
11. Serve hot.

Miscellaneous

Chicken Stock

Method

1. Place all the ingredients in a stockpot.
2. Cover with cold water.
3. Bring to a boil over high heat. Remove any impurities that rise to the top.
4. Reduce the heat and simmer the stock for 3–4 hours.
5. Taste for the strength of stock you want. Put away from the heat.
6. Let the stock sit for 10–15 minutes, then ladle through a fine strainer.
7. Remove the fat from the stock by skimming with a ladle.
8. Cool by placing the container of strained stock in an ice water bath, then refrigerate.
9. Use whenever required.

Ingredients

2.25 kgs chicken bones
1 large onion, peeled and quartered
2 large or 4 small leeks (or spring onions), cut in half lengthwise and well washed
2 bay leaves
6 sprigs of fresh flat-leaf parsley (or coriander leaves)
½ tsp dried thyme (optional)
12 whole black peppercorns

French Dressing

Ingredients

1	tsp salt
½	tsp sugar
¼	tsp pepper
1	clove garlic, minced
½	tsp red chilli powder
⅓	cup vinegar
⅔	cup olive oil

Method

1. Combine all the ingredients and shake well in a covered jar. Store in the refrigerator. Shake well before using.

Garam Masala

Method

1. Roast the cumin seeds till brown.
2. Heat all the other ingredients slightly so that they do not have any moisture.
3. Grind together to a fine powder.
4. Store in an air-tight jar and use whenever you feel like.

Tip : You can experiment with this masala by adding or subtracting ingredients based on the dish you are cooking.

Ingredients

15 gm Cinnamon
10 gm Cardamom
10 gm Cloves
50 gm Cumin Seed
10 gm Bay leaf
10 gm Ginger
10 gm Green Cardamom
5 gm Pepper Black
Salt to taste

Vegetable Stock

Ingredients

2 medium potatoes, thickly chopped
2 shallots (red onions), skins removed and quartered
2 spring onions, chopped into 0.5"pieces; remove the very root ends, but include the green leaves
3–4 medium carrots (unpeeled), thickly chopped
3–5 garlic cloves, peeled and cut in half
A couple of handfuls of unchopped coriander leaves
9–12black peppercorns
1–2 bay leaves, crumbled
1 apple or pear, quartered
1 sweet potato optional
3.5 lt water

Method

1. Put the peppercorns, coriander leaves and bay leaves into a large pot.
2. Put in the rest of the ingredients.
3. Pour in the water to cover the ingredients.
4. Bring to a boil and let simmer for about 1 hour. Cool and strain to remove any pieces of vegetables, fruit or scraps. Add salt and its ready to use.

Sour Cream

Ingredients

1 cup cream

1½ cups pasteurized whole milk

½ cup buttermilk

Method

1. Mix all the ingredients in a bowl over warm water.
2. Raise the temperature of the mixture to about 20°C and let it stand for 12 to 24 hours or until it is sufficiently sour and thick enough to cling firmly to a spoon.
3. Keep in the refrigerator until you want to use it.
4. For a richer heavier sour cream combine 2 cups of pasteurized heavy cream with 5 tablespoons of cultured buttermilk and incubate as before. For better texture refrigerate for 24 hours before serving.

Tip : Hang fresh curds in muslin cloth for 10 minutes. Add milk if necessary to get consistency for surprisingly similar results.

Coconut Milk

Ingredients

Fresh coconut

Method

1. Grate the white flesh of a brown coconut using a cheese grater (the fine side will produce better results).
2. Add one cup of warm water to the grated coconut, put in a bowl and squeeze with your hands or put in a food processor and blitz.
3. Put results in a fine muslin cloth, twist into a ball and squeeze as hard as you can. The first results are the thickest, called coconut cream. The second and third cup of water you add and squeeze results in coconut milk which is thinner.

Glossary

Aloo	:	Potato
Garam Masala	:	Ground Spices
Gobhi	:	Cauliflower
Mirchi	:	Chilli
Moong	:	Legume–Green
Paneer	:	Cottage Cheese

Basmati rice :

Basmati rice is authentic Indian long grained white rice, which has unique nutty flavor. Basmati rice is very popular in India and all over the world. A wide variety of rice dishes are made with Basmati rice. They are: plain steamed rice, pulaos, pilafs, biryanis or just different types of fried rice – which include meat, vegetables, nuts, and even fruits sometimes. Gourmet cooks prefer to use Basmati rice for its fragrant flavor. Special occasion rice dishes are mostly made with Basmati rice.

Biryani :

Elaborate dish made from spiced saffron rice cooked with pieces of lamb, chicken or vegetables. It is usually made on special occasions since it takes a long time to make a biryani, but it is surely worth the effort. It always tastes better the next day since the spices marinate and flavor the meat and rice.

Chaat :

Salty snacks served with an array of sweet and spicy chutneys.

Dal :

Dal is an Indian word, which includes dried peas, beans, and lentils which are red, yellow orange, or pink, plus split peas and other legumes. Dal can also be used to describe a soup like dish prepared with lentils. Dals are the primary source of protein in a vegetarian diet. Dals are cooked whole or pureed, depending on the dish. Ground powdered dal is used in unleavened breads and crackers, and even in spice mixtures.

Glossary

Dum :

A way to steam foods in a pot with a tightly covered lid or a sealed pot. A popular spiced vegetable dish is "Dum Aloo". In the olden days, the utensil was sealed with atta (dough) to capture the moisture within the food as it cooked slowly over a charcoal fire. Some coal was placed on the lid to ensure even cooking. The food continued to cook in its own steam, retaining all its flavour and aroma. Dum means, "to steam" or "maute" a dish.

Gosht :

Meat generic. This could be either lamb or beef.

Halwa :

Indian sweet made from a variety of finely grated vegetables, milk and sugar and flavored with cardamom. The consistency is that of a thick pudding. Among the popular Halwa is the "Gajar Halwa".

Khoya :

Also known as "mawa" is made by bringing milk to a boil in a pot and stirring continuously thereafter on a low flame. It is then reduced and thickened to the consistency of soft cream cheese. Used widely in the making of many Indian desserts and sweet meats.

Korma :

Rich sauce thickned with yogurt, nuts or poppy seeds.

Masala :

Spices, herbs and other seasonings ground or pounded together. When wet ingredients like water, vinegar, yogurt etc. are added to the spice mixture it is appropriately called a "wet masala". Dry spice mixtures are also called "Garam masala" or commonly known in the world as "Curry powder". Indian cooks generally don't use pre-prepared curry power - originally a British invention to approximate Indian seasoning - but prefer making their own ever changing blends.

Glossary

Mysore Pak :

It is a sweet dish of Karnataka, usally served as dessert. it is made of generous amounts of ghee (clarified butter), sugar and chick pea (besan) flour.

Naan :

Indian flat bread made from wheat and baked in a tandoor.

Rasgulla :

One of the most famous Indian sweets that originated from east India. The balls made from milk are cooked in a light sugar syrup, flavored with cardamom. Served chilled.

Deep-fried cake balls served with aromatic syrups.

Sambhar :

Lentil curry form the south of India. Served as an accompaniment with "idli" and "dosa".

Tandoor :

The traditional Indian clay oven is called the "Tandoor". A Tandoor is a clay pot usually sunken neck deep in the ground. Charcoal is put on the flat bottom of the pot. The heat generated by the hot charcoal in and on the sides of the clay pot is used for cooking. Long iron rods, long enough to reach the bottom of the pot, are used in the cooking process. It is probably the most versatile kitchen equipment in the Indian kitchen. Barbecues, breads, dal, gravies made in them acquire a unique taste, very different from the food cooked on the regular kitchen oven.

Tandoori Gobhi :

Cauliflower marinated with spices, red color and yogurt, cooked in a tandoor. Try making it as described in the cook book or at your favorite restaurant.

Glossary

English	Hindi

Dry Fruits and Fruits

English	Hindi
Almonds	Badam
Apricot	Khubani
Cashewnuts	Kaju
Dried dates	Chuare
Dried fruits	Sukha Mewa
Fresh cream	Malai
Pistachio	Pista
Banana	Kela
Banana leaf	Kele ka patta
Betel nut	Supari
Black grapes	Kale angoor
Blueberries	Falsa
Berries	Ker
Coconut	Nariyal
Custard apple	Sharifa/Sitaphal
Dates	Khajur
Dried beans	Sangri
Fresh pomegranate pearls	Anar ke dane
Grapes	Angoor
Indian gooseberry	Amla
Lemon	Nimboo
Mango	Aam

English	Hindi
Musk Melon	Kharbooj
Peaches	Aadoo

Grains & Pulses

Barley	Jau
Basmati rice	Basmati chawal
Bengal gram flour	Besan
Corn kernels	Makai ke dane
Cornmeal	Makai ka atta
Finger millet	ragi/nachni
Flattened rice	Poha/chewra
Gram flour	Besan
Sago	Sabudana
Semolina	Rawa/Sooji
Sweetcorn kernels	Makai ke dane
Bean sprouts	Ankurit moong
Black Bengal gram	Kale chane
Black eyed beans	Lobia
Broad beans	Papdi
Chickpeas	Kabuli chana
Cluster beans	Guar
Green gram dumplings	Mangodi
Kidney beans	Rajma

English	Hindi
Pigeon peas	Sabut toovar/ Sabut arhar
Split Bengal gram	Chana dal
Split black gram skinless	Dhuli urad dal
Split black gram with skin	Chilkewali urad dal
Split coriander seeds	Dhania dal
Split fenugreek seeds	Methi dal
Split green gram skinless	Dhuli moong dal
Split green gram with skin	Chilkewali moong dal
Split lentils	Masoor dal
Split pigeon peas	Toovar dal/Arhar dal
Sprouted green gram	Ankurit moong
Whole black gram	Sabut urad
Whole green gram	Sabut moong
Whole red lentils	Sabut masoor

Herbs and Spices

Celery	Ajmud
Fresh basil	Tulsi
Fresh coriander	Hara dhania
Fresh mint	Pudina
Fresh parsely	Ajmoda

English	Hindi
Fresh turmeric	Tazi haldi
Aniseed	Saunf
Asafoetida	Hing
Bay leaf	Tej patta
Black cardamoms	Badi elaichi
Black peppercorns	Kali mirch
Black salt	Kala namak
Camphor	Kapur
Caraway seeds	Shahi jeera
Carom seeds	Ajwain
Cinnamon	dalchini
Cloves	Laung
Coriander powder	Dhania powder
Coriander seeds	Sabut Dhania
Cumin seeds	Jeera
Curry leaves	Kadhi patta/ meetha neem
Dried pomegranate seeds	Anardana
Dried red chillies	Sookhi lal mirch
Dried coconut	Khopra
Dried ginger powder	Saunth
Dried fenugreek leaves	Kasoori methi
Dried mango powder	Amchur
Fennel seeds	Saunf

Glossary

Glossary

English	Hindi
Green cardamoms	Chhoti elaichi
Mace	Javitri
Mustard seeds	Rai/sarson
Nutmeg	Jaiphal
Onion seeds	Kalonji
Sesame seeds	Til
Split mustard seeds	Rai dal
Star anise	Chakri Phool/ Badiyan
Turmeric powder	Haldi powder

Vegetables, Poultry and Others

Aubergine/Eggplant/Brinjal	Baingan
Avocado	Makhanphal
Baby brinjals	Chhote baingan
Baby potatoes	Chhote aloo
Beetroot	Chukandar
Bitter gourd	Karela
Bottle gourd	Lauki/ghia/doodhi
Brinjal	Baingan
Browned onion	Bhuna pyaaz
Cabbage	Pattagobhi

English	Hindi
Carrots	Gajar
Cauliflower	Phoolgobhi
Cherry tomatoes	Chhote tamatar
Cucumber	Kakdi/Kheera
Drumsticks	Saijan ki Phalli
Eggplants	Baingan
Fenugreek leaves	Methi
French beans	Farsi
Fresh red chillies	Tazi lal mirch
Garlic	Lehsun
Ginger	Adrak
Green capsicum	Hari Shimla mirch
Green chillies	Hari mirch
Green peas	Matar
Jackfruit	Kathal
Ladyfingers	Bhindi
Leek	Bilayti pyaaz
Lotus roots	Kamal kakdi/Bhen
Mushrooms	Kukurmutta/Gucchi/ Dhingri/Khumb
Onions	Pyaaz
Peanuts/ground nuts	Moongphali
Potatoes	Aloo
Red cabbage	Lal gobhi

Glossary

English	Hindi
Red capsicum	Lal Shimla mirch
Red pumpkin	Kaddu
Spinach	Palak
Spring onion	Hara pyaaz
Sweet potato	Shakkarkand/ Rattalu
Tomatoes	Tamatar
Zucchini	Tori/Turaii
Chicken	Murgh
Chicken breasts	Murgh ka seena
Chicken mince	Murgh keema
Chicken wings and shoulder	Murgh pankhari
Bean curd	Tofu
Citric acid	Tartri
Cottage cheese	Paneer
Jaggery	Gur
Mustard oil	Rai ka tel/ Sarson ka tel
Tamarind	Imli
Tea leaves	Chai ki pattiyan